www.finishinglinepress.com

Holy Week
in
Cave Country

poems by

Kimberly Sailor

Finishing Line Press
Georgetown, Kentucky

Holy Week
in
Cave Country

Publisher: Leah Huete de Maines
Editor: Christen Kincaid
Cover Art: Adam Sailor
Author Photo: Kimberly Sailor
Cover Design: Elizabeth Maines McCleavy

Order online: www.finishinglinepress.com
also available on amazon.com

Author inquiries and mail orders:
Finishing Line Press
PO Box 1626
Georgetown, Kentucky 40324
USA

Contents

To Adam, my mild-mannered computer programmer.
Hey: thanks for building the scaffolding right under my feet.

Soft Land is Dangerous for Livestock

Southwest Kentucky? Karst topography.
Ominous sinkholes: acne pocks in the middle of cow-strewn fields.
Will the bovine fall through the spongy soil? What if the cows cluster,
stampede, all drawn to the same sunken divot
for just the right cuds of springy alfalfa, or a family's
forgotten berry basket, from thickets that grow

like tavern dart leagues, heavy and sticky
when there's not much going down, which is always
in southwest Kentucky. Your ticketed show
remains underground, where healing huts for the rich
were built in the 1800s. Cave air cures all, except
for tuberculosis. Cave owners shouldn't advertise miracles.

Caves aren't Jesus, and they don't pretend to be.
Neglecting the farmer's warnings, the cows do gather,
over bread and wine, imported
because big heifers produce neither, standing tail to shoulder
inside round circles on the ground.
If we spray paint the edges, the sinkholes

are probably six feet apart; close enough, anyway.
Safe enough, if the heifers don't chuff hot gossip.
But then it happens: cattle break through
the limestone layers under-hoof, their startled calls and hide spots
smacking the air, fleshy udder bags spinning and spraying
fresh high-fat cream until cows land in cave country below.

The newly formed entrance: a little rough, not quite
up to fire codes, but a profitable attraction stand
for curious tourists who heard about the cows
and want a brief peek before church.
And if beef flanks can break through the terrain,
just fall through on an idle Sunday,

so can we. Now the cows have to create
a new underground community,
uniquely patterned mole-steins. Eventually,
they will succumb to the dark.
It is not Ordinary Times:
our country is delicate, and wild.

We fight over cotton cloth
and tenderize public education with metal mallets.
Mealy-mouthed: lower ropes to the cows,
join a many-miles
Eastertide pilgrimage to Kentucky, during
the most curious of Holy Weeks.

Travel Dress

modern-fit Hawaiian shirts
neon flamingos in floaties, buzzy and doped up
from smoking the hemp fabric
of corporate hippies

it's because of the organic cucumber people
that we got into this mess
trying to perfect
God's free garden

seeds in my pocket, germ-
inating to the Heavens
waving sunflower stalks
out of Levis, denim heads

on fire, green manure-rich
spires tickling the tourists
who float close,
inspecting my family field, wondering: how come?

how safe can it be, to recklessly wander
the United States
with yellow-petal daughters
trailing behind me?

Backed Up in Louisville, Where I Used to Date an Opera Singer

Just serve ham and colored eggs in April, so any metro-minded cows
are excused from the communion line.

Nearing-the-end-of-covid-maybe-fucking-please plans: a national park,
driving range. We are responsible, recycling Americans

who cannot lasso airport alamos, but desire
the literal homeland. The economy: stretching, sore and knotted

after an unexpected recliner nap during Jeopardy!—federally funded fun
is pretty clean, with organized tours hourly

and decent accommodations for families of four. Starting point:
Mount Horeb, Wisconsin; an activist sort of place, but too familiar,

tightly contained. Destination:
Mammoth Cave, Kentucky.

Qualifying for national park status: tricky and political, slippery
savage origins. Sing *Hamilton* and know; hey, I dated an opera singer!

With me: a tech husband who codes; the older daughter who tested
three years ahead in math yet holds her piss so long she grabs

her crotch and stomps; and the younger girl, who lives to loudly
disagree but is so enjoyable that everyone tolerates her shit because

she warms and snugs the night air, a tightly spun chrysalis, ready
to burst life particles, photons of ombre light, which you won't find

in any cave, national or otherwise. Forbidden within: petrol, firewood
from blue states, soy candles, imported batteries, takeout or

Dollar Store pop tarts (eat in the cafeteria with a 685% mark-up,
you unpatriotic heathen), quiet hopes, bleached paper journals,

national anthem recordings by black hip hop artists who frolic
around the melody instead of getting right to the metered point,

hot plates from China, pets of any stripe, or giving problems to anyone
but the official complaint form—translated in Spanish upon request—

which must be mailed outside the park grounds because who
has the staff to handle your nonsense, much less solve your problem?

Halfway down, arrested in cerebral crisis: what is a park?
Does it require grass? Benches? Boundaries? Ball diamonds?

Zones for the dog to shit, no glass policies, boulders for kids
to break bones upon? Is that homeless vet really selling

succulents on the Louisville expressway? So trendy
are those waxy, boxy sprouts, even the antique store

peddles them. If it weren't for you
marking time in this new age SUV with me,

I wouldn't know if we were anxious
Spring Break parents, or morse code operators

living in WWII. Mammoth Cave was excavated for saltpeter by slaves,
which just might change your notion of compound elements.

The Depression Tray

I cannot pack lightly
      for I carry heavy things

two feet by three feet
      industrial grade melamine

a trendy teal platter that does not hold
      soup and crackers, tea service, or pulpy juice

an uppity faux French Country piece
      affordably rides in cargo or overhead, slumbers late in hotels

I bring this synthetic rectangle everywhere,
      premenstrual herbs and nerve calmers look fancy, put-together

this depression tray wasn't born in Housewares
      a plastics factory, or the slaughterhouse; it began here

I carry it under-arm like a surfboard, down corridors, between
      hedgerows, catching my autobiography before splattering

across mixed-use lanes. I carry this constant, I carry its history,
      to avoid a dangerous confrontation, with me.

Perhaps It's Viral

One crimson, pus-filled boil, atop the un-nailed skin
of my left-hand rib cage. A bump not close enough to
underwire for irritation. Not a crown of thorns corset.
Popped up overnight, after a sneaker-run down the
Green River bluffs. Not burstable. Search with weak
WiFi: *covid symptoms*. No matches, but if you need
pro-vaccine support in your traditional family, show them:
smallpox photos, children, twin hospital beds, arranged in
easy-flow rows, thirty black and white first graders with
wart-filled faces, lumpy lips and eyeballs crusted closed,
out of school and in pain, shoelace-tying lessons suspended,
white-hatted nurses holding fluid bags and bloody rags.
This is not your historic bug, or tiny tick bite. Not itchy, stingy,
scabby. I'll self-heal without Dollar Store meds or Facebook
crystals, because I keep my lungs clear, the organs beneath
the feet of my mammary glands. But in case this is from
the woods, or seed-floated across state lines, and because I am
a responsible, recycling American, moderately invested in
preventing the spread of infectious diseases, I call the ranger
station. A man named Marty, past retirement age, summons
me over *after the morning rush*. Mysterious, so I prepare for
the diagnosis bazaar. Marty rubs a finger over the fester, not
to be dirty, just thorough, digits coated with pine shavings
because he has to prune along the trails even though that's
clearly Don's job. The grand poobah of national park care
squints and declares: *Huh, dunno. Everyone has an opinion.*
Husband suspects an allergic reaction, *maybe the lodge soap*,
as though I am washing a one-inch by one-inch surface only
on my filthy, forgotten rib cage skin that produces one lonely
pus-filled zit. Can't be frisky with no room to swing a cat,
so admittedly, not a lot of soap or landscaping needed,
but let's think critically here. The middle school scientist:
*a compromised immune system / you might have HIV /
that comes before AIDS.* The young pop-off: *is it red marker?
Don't sleep with the cap off.* On the antenna-reliant television,
a portly weatherman suggests *good sleeping weather*, while I sit

criss-crossed and uncrease a takeout menu discovered behind the radiator, a machine hissing and banging for unbiased mechanical attention while waiting for its dose of antiviral spike protein prevention.

Four Quarters: A Contemporary Sonnet

Wait days to lantern-blaze into sacred underground spaces
for long is the ticket queue and short are the workers;
the once-packed suitcase already empty, turned over, dug through
for name-brand snacks, and no denim shorts, no cotton shoelaces.

And so, to the Dollar Store you go. We heard Easter Week
would be cool-temped, like the cave Mary shrouded Jesus in,
but that was simply: a lie. A door poster shouts about an egg hunt
Saturday: we will go. Religiously and culturally and calorically.

We hop to generic pop tarts, and that's when she rises, unisex smock
drooping off pointy shoulders. The Clerk, permed, boasting
half-priced tampons and pregnancy tests. She boxes last fall's
pumpkins and ghosts, a real steal at a quarter, for quarterly numbers.

So long, to the working women of Hart County.
So long, until our turn.

How do you break up a day o' biding?

How do you break up a day o' biding?
A car ferry hauls one rusted-out ashtray
athwart Kentucky's beatnik brown, Green River.

A non-float boat, metal pulleys rolling
since 1934, save Christmas Day.
How do you break up a day o' biding?

So short the passage, two ferry-lengths long
walk on water, faster the miracle
athwart Kentucky's beatnik brown, Green River.

Quaint, free history: tavern dart leagues
cattle auctions, mole subterraneans.
How do you break up a day o' biding?

A kayaker pushes out everything:
a couple's trip last March, solo this spring
athwart Kentucky's beatnik brown, Green River.

Stop engine, set break. Is it in the waiting,
or in the motion, that we vacation?
How do you break up a day o' biding
athwart Kentucky's beatnik brown, Green River?

Shark Teeth in Mammoth Cave

1. My daughter talks about Heaven so casually,
you'd think she visits after school.

She is the unicorn of believers: Jesus in her veins
fossil DNA on her brain.

this is what happens, when raised across denominations
with a hymn-singing mama, and data scientist dad.

2. Only one show running,
The Discovery Tour. It's finally our turn in Cave Country.

Tightly roped, confined and controlled
like black Welsh cattle in feed stalls

getting heavy on what we give them, and in this cave,
one tight passage called Fat Man's Misery.

3. Stephen Bishop, the rail-thin enslaved black man
made the first Mammoth maps,

roped down to new places alone;
led the silk-buttoned people with his sooty oil lantern,

described the caverns to the curious 1830s world as:
grand, gloomy, peculiar.

4. Bishop created a tourist sensation, a demand for regional rails
and the right to walk with Him, the geological shepherd.

Stephen received a second-hand tombstone at the Park,
his name chiseled after a Civil War family never paid for the slab.

5. My child, the believer-scientist, rattles off how many passageways
we're missing due to social distance restrictions, like on a normal year

we'd just Razor scooter all 420 miles, dynamite and cafeteria
ice cream in hand. It's muddy for limestone, and relentlessly rowdy

for a national park. I remind myself that reverence is saved
for national cemeteries. But today, is Maundy Thursday.

6. We are holy wonderment ambassadors, guides like Bishop
to overseas tourists who arrive by new machines

wearing masks instead of petticoats;
though there's enough stereotypes about the American South

without having this father from Alabama
joke if there's a pissing corner.

7. I am rattled, grandly irritated, gloomy and peculiar myself,
looking back to see if streaks of surface light

from the waterfall-enveloped entrance
can bore a path through history.

Did you know this cave
has 1830s graffiti? Creatively thin: the line between artist and vandal.

8. There are stopping stations
where men and women in Indiana Jones khaki

deliver sixty-second scripts, rehearsed sermons
on artifacts, discoveries, and death.

One station, just for kids,
near a cross-shaped display

of tiny fingerprinted magnifying glasses;
study aids for budding speleologists.

9. The khaki-preacher waves us over
flips on a flashlight and fishes out

a shark puppet, its silhouette
black and bouncing on mineral-rich walls.

10. *What's this?* he asks
my kids, who reply with a hesitant

Ugh-shark? to which he nods
with satisfaction, his customers

following the orchestration. The light beam shoots up
illuminating a dull triangle patch on the cave's ceiling.

11. *What's this?* he asks again.
The believer-scientist squints skyward,

still a few seasons away from glasses.
Her little sister declares, *A tooth!*

sticking a hangnail finger into her mouth
while the elder sister answers, "That's a shark tooth …

in Kentucky." Her spirit
unmoors itself from her rib cage

pushing out her young pores
before floating away in curled wispy soul-smoke

to a place no one will ever map, while the khaki-preacher
smugly states: *over 40 species down here!*

12. Years later, when we are both different,
on an unassuming Thursday

I will ask her:
When did you stop believing in God?

and she will say,
The day I saw the shark teeth.

Break Up the Day with Kangaroos

every exit in southwest Kentucky
a coiffed cultural experience of life-sized dinosaurs,
ziplines and minigolf, to ground yourself
if the rich geology, simply overwhelms

> to date, there is no font
> for sarcasm
> and exotic wildlife laws
> are on the lam, too

on sandy slopes
we are knee-deep in lounging marsupials
my youngest: they are so sleepy
the eldest: they are so drugged

> as usual, reality
> keeps the wolf from the door:
> tickets are pricey
> but we merrily stroke Australian fur

charmed and suspended between pleasure and covid
we feed rainbow lorikeets dixie cups of sugar water
their gray segmented feet
delicately curled around fat human thumbs

> cartwheeling paper trash
> piles up in pens like lab studies
> but my pictures, my felicity,
> my semi-responsible American existence

here, before we go
a lively sheep herding show
and a surprisingly sparkly Cave of Wonders
neither gloomy or peculiar, included with the day's admission

if you are fortunate enough to find caves
below your family's foundation, or happen upon
a pregnant kangaroo to start a full-pouched empire,
I beg you: Jesus, don't waste your life.

For Marty, in Darkness

On days when the Kentucky
bourbon sweats, I see you park
the tractor, hang the chain on a gas-powered
push mower, because you like labor
harder than it has to be.

Trail report conditions, written inside
on the plushiest part of a red-letter Thursday:
pastel twilight, on popular Sunset Ridge.
Some forgo the limestone caves
just for this capstone view;

two hikers brought state-line champagne,
clinking while you eat your dinner
two hundred yards back
in a splintered maintenance shed
that will only survive

with robust hand-sanding. Dry ham
on gas station croissants, no sauce;
that's all the way
in that other guy's fridge, the ass
who never applies sealant right.

Your grass clippings look up
to catch the damn day's end,
emptied in a brush pile
with blinking green eyes, searching
for a way out of the compost

before the middle heats up,
and the breakdown begins.
I see your Coleman lantern
flicks off at ten. Someone's black lab
is chuffed from chipmunk chasing

under the postcard magnolia trees
that only bloom in four trim lines
for three undying April days
and I have to ask: are you happy?

Minutes from The Reason You Came

The NPS will take this one when the water finally bursts through to Mammoth's officially mapped domain. Eventually they will all connect, all the caves in America, though we know there are many more caves under the ocean because families of sharks have to live somewhere. When unification happens, we will all sink down together, wet and bewildered below seven new continent islands. I'll be deliriously smug about the extra legroom on a previously overpopulated planet, because I get like that sometimes. Hey: it will take a while to gather our sensibilities, so don't expect a hot meal unless you know which kind of rocks retain heat. That's a specialty kind of cooking, not on the usual celebrity chef shows.

There are wet caves and dry caves, like seasons on the seven islands we just tipped overboard from, the ones that used to hold latin beats and leggy dancers the further south you rowed. Not all of us will make it through the natural disaster, but there won't be newspapers to run obituaries, at least not right away. I am a poet, but if I lose you, I'll gently say, *I'm sorry for my loss.*

Cheap caves surround Mammoth with no lines, because if there's a nearby anchor attraction to profit from, let's get this shit done. And all the clearance-priced Dollar Store caves are wet, which means they are very pretty in addition to being a smashing value, even if you don't have a senior citizen or military discount. Mammoth is dry, for now. The water eventually takes back everything. We know that because of the shark teeth. But modern history! Mammoth is scandalous and oddly sad for a rock tunnel, so we forgive all the monotone beige because it has a good story, and again, it's just so very large. When will it end?

Some Kentucky caves come with billboards to make sure you're aware there's limitless spelunking, as though you could forget with new sinkholes proudly waving from the fields and parking lots after their evening smoke. I don't recall how Hidden River Cave is advertised, but here's my brochure: you enter on sturdy steel fishing steps that descend down a craggy asteroid pit in someone's former backyard. The whole thing was purchased by a private owner to be a legit cave licensed with the county, dirt chunks sometimes crumbling off as you descend from daylight. For an extra fifteen bucks you can repel down to the bottom. It's really incredible, they'll strap a bike helmet on you with a round light, which makes your selfies extremely authentically adventurey. Complimentary high wader boots too, in many sizes. Something will fit you.

Turns out the river is not hidden, and at times it's a waist-high, roaring persona of power-making urgency before it slims down to the same stodgy waterway that holds that damn historic car ferry. The fish down here are white with no eyeballs, because let's get freaky. Get ready: you have to walk right through the river, while taking your screaming kids piggyback who yell *more, more, this is awesome,* and nobody cares about the yelling, because it really is awesome. Turns out the adventure helmets and waders are not for show: they are necessary equipment. I should have suspected as much when we signed up for a tour on a clipboard with a guy who is conveniently a volunteer firefighter.

Once, a geology class from a nearby college got stuck in the back section for two days until the river went down below neck-level; the owner was forced to hardwire an emergency response phone after that, which surely made the stuffy professionals at Mammoth frown because they don't take risks with guest safety and really, that kind of shit colors the experience for all of us who care for the region and care for mother earth.

The world's longest underground suspension bridge is down here, too, but funny, the water is pretty shallow over that section. What an enticing finger-beckoning: *walk across the longest, baby.* Can my brochure fit in a plug for the soaring dome in the cave? The ceiling is much higher than it looks; a chapel for Easter worship, an echo chamber for kids to yell obscenities and have them ring back to mom and dad's ears in triplets, *fuck fuck fuck.* Can't recall when I've had this much fun.

Good Friday,
was a different kind of holy.

Tiny Thieves in the Ovum Tomb

Sacred Silverado pulls into park grounds
a wooden cross bed-rests, made from 2x4s
industrially stapled the night before

performing preacher-man, regional celebrity,
punches the sky, wrecks a loaf of homemade
sourdough across the truck's grill, savage

but regionally relatable, because we're all
beasts for Jesus down here.
Die, rise, his body ridin' in that crew cab.

Young, un-nailed hands pray for mountain bikes,
three-wheel trikes, specialty snowboards for sand,
wheely skateboards for caves, free tickets

to the kangaroo zoo, bigger prizes if you go
to church tomorrow—eternal life winnings,
no golden egg or raffle ticket needed—

all generously donated. He is risen,
He is risen indeed
given onto

You. An uncomfortable skit: red paint on white
sheets. Are we still talking about His death or my
murder if I interfere with the locals

dying, rising, His body ridin'.
Laundry baskets of eggs, Dollar Store pastels,
whipped onto Kentucky's bluegrass for collection,

so plush even with poverty and rogue pickup
parking, more red paint, thrown skyward, hysteria
in fake blood, shed for us and staining our ivory lids.

Someone hums that famous song: *no colors anymore*
I want them to turn black
children laughing, hopping, breaking spines of hymnals,

tossing tithings into a trucker's cap passed from the right,
listening for the countdown, salivating for uneaten
chocolate, but the hype man leads us in more prayer,

more frenzied fire, because poultry adoration
and color symbolism can wait when Jesus
died for us. Remember: all of this will be given

onto you, when you eat Him, when you yearn
for Him. Stay hungry, stuff the broken shells
into hoodies and hats

when the baskets are full, because the church
don't have no storage space for aging AirHeads.
Just one more thing, before you collect from

the tomb of life: don't wear no more masks neither,
not ever, because the Lord is your Savior. Faith
over fear. Cheers and bloody high-fives from the skit

actors, and then, the blessing
to go.

Two brothers, Peterson boys who live north
of the Green River, didn't come back to school
'cause they got covid from trading

wet bites of Twix. But they lived free, only killed
one uncle from their coughing, and played
lots of Mario Kart in the karst topography

of God-gripped Kentucky.

Review of Mammoth Lodge
K. Skinner, Chicago, IL. TOP REVIEWER.

The bathroom is undergoing an identity crisis—70s yellow with red art deco, are you high right now? I follow snazzy home blogs; time has pinned this bathroom down in a butterfly net. The low-pressure shower head offers but a trickle, slowly strangling itself, spitting out blobby tears upon a tired traveler's chest. The bed? Appropriate for neither sleep nor sex, both being too uncomfortable to discuss in the characters permitted. Temperature regulation? You're better off sleeping in the damn cave because at least that's stable. Thankful to my Lord and Savior that sweating burns calories, which management will be doing after reading this review from a certified influencer. I've stayed all over, even filthy New York; such a shame about our national parks, no one cares anymore. The groundskeeper is creepy, too. How often do you have to check on guests? I am tired of him and tired from this dusty-ass lodge. —KS

our youngest twirls a storm-colored emu feather
she thieved from a cage
at the kangaroo zoo

my husband,
supine with a pop-science novel about time travel
receives a suggestive spousal text:

Wanna code a real-world fix, hot stuff?
I need cow shit deleted, forever.
The kids can watch:

just make the process educational
in the name of societal advancement
instead of federal-land criminal.

When We Lived

I stay awake the longest
because it takes a while to forget

younger-you: no kids, pre-beard
enough energy to sling trash bags

on Church Sponsored Sundays along
rural highways, slow-cooking

venison that your dad shot, dead
in an unremarkable fall.

I stay awake the longest:
time alone to grieve non-applicable scripture

in a room full of patterned sleep-breathers:
too choppy for peace, too close for data-noted loss.

Sadness pings the radiator. Sonar
can't detect first graders, misinterprets fifth graders.

This is no way for them to grow up,
suspended in a partial proverb-broken life.

In an ocean of federal blips on park screens,
the sonar instrument finds me, maps me, copies me

then distributes me in shop boutiques, clearly labeled
reproduction. I have not seen deer here, only rabbits,

but this is not remarkable; this is not
Ordinary Times.

Haven't slept in the woods since I was a kid. I'll never
see you chop a cord, because that's not you.

Easter Sunday in a Tow Truck

Bunny ears, bunny ears, playing by a tree
criss-cross, criss-cross, try to catch me

Holy are the miles on foot.
Learning to run at forty felt
perfectly thrilling during a pandemic:

is this my escape hatch?
Get as far as I can
while teachers yell at kids encased in squares?

I leave my family
tucked into the knothole of a county park.
Northern Indiana: the great equalizer—

miles from anywhere, so you'd better
have a backup plan or a good stretch
before an interstate blowout.

Everything is closed on Easter Sunday
but I believe overtime Holiday Pay
brings Christians to their knees.

No one answers the mechanic's phone
but I believe in desperate traveler
new tire inflation, at least twice the price on Sundays.

The tow truck driver, maskless
with an unlit Camel between sticky Cadbury lips,
tells me I'm crazy, reckless

to run five miles just to check, just in case.
What about muggers, muscle cramps? I shrug
because there are no sinkholes in Northern Indiana.

I share vacation photos; his kids would love
underground rivers, fossils on ceilings.
We talk about our own caves; the temples,

the sanctuaries we promise to fix up
a little better now, and I confess
this is how faith works.

Kimberly Sailor, from Mount Horeb, Wisconsin, studied creative writing at the University of Southern California and is the editor-in-chief of the Recorded A Cappella Review Board. She is a 2020 poetry fellowship recipient from the Martha's Vineyard Institute of Creative Writing; a 2019 and 2022 Hal Prize poetry finalist; and 2023 Wisconsin People & Ideas finalist. Her poetry has appeared in *Driftwood Press, Sixfold, the Peninsula Pulse, Silver Birch Press,* and *Eunoia Review.* Sailor is the author of the novel *The Clarinet Whale*, stays active on education boards, and serves as a Firefighter/EMT across communities. She ferociously loves her quirky family, running laps around town, her pickup truck Big Red, and thinking about bigfoot.

kimberlysailor.com

www.ingramcontent.com/pod-product-compliance
Lightning Source LLC
Chambersburg PA
CBHW022059080426
42734CB00009B/1413